First published 2019 in Macmillan by Pan Macmillan Australia Pty Ltd
1 Market Street, Sydney, New South Wales, Australia, 2000

Concept and text copyright © Petra James 2019
Illustration copyright © Alissa Dinallo 2019

Cataloguing-in-Publication entry is available
from the National Library of Australia
http://catalogue.nla.gov.au

Cover by Alissa Dinallo

Printed in China by 1010 Printing International Limited

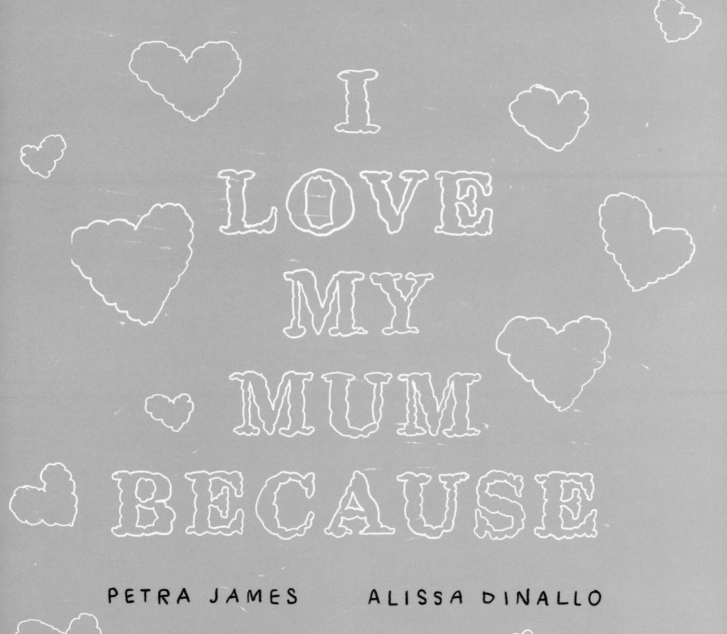

I LOVE MY MUM BECAUSE

PETRA JAMES   ALISSA DINALLO

Macmillan
Pan Macmillan Australia

Me and

♥ Draw a picture of you.

my mum

♥ Draw a picture of your mum.

I
love
my
mum
because

She gives me
the stars

Count the stars in this night sky.

and the
moon.

Answer → 85

She was little once
upon a time . . .

mum

My

♥ Draw a line to connect each
little shape to its big shape, then
add some words about your mum.

is

_____

_____

_____

so she knows
what it's like.

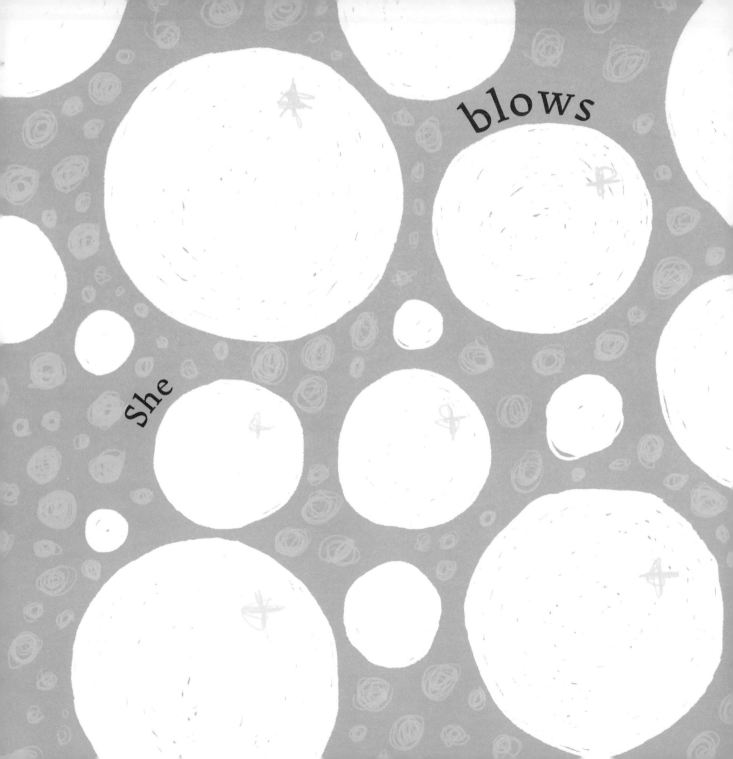

BUBBLES!

♥ Write a wish
or two inside the
bubbles. Close your
eyes and blow
the wish away.

She

brings

♥ Colour in the flowers
to create the brightest
bunch for your mum.

me

Spring.

She

hides

and

I

seek.

♥ Spot the mum.

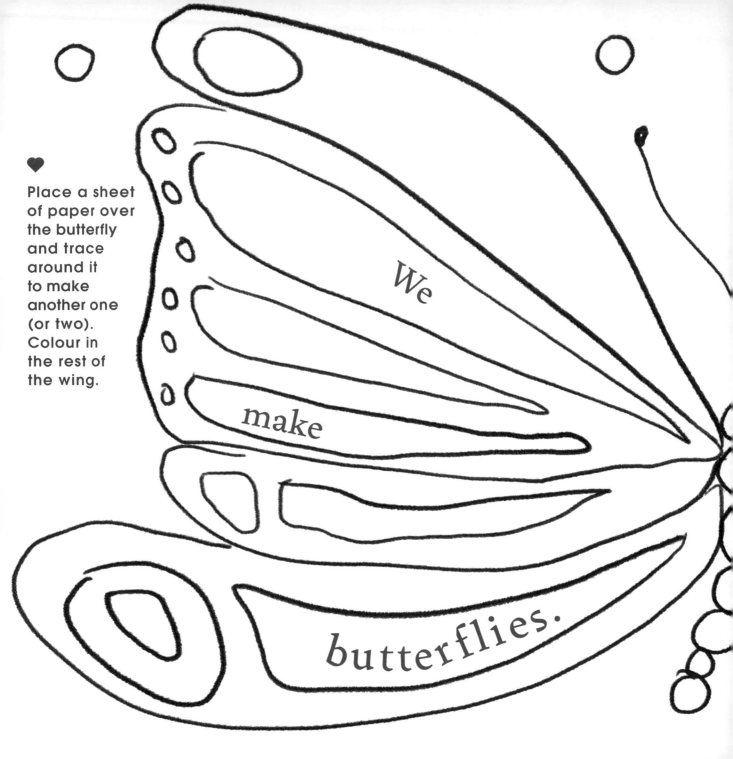

Place a sheet of paper over the butterfly and trace around it to make another one (or two). Colour in the rest of the wing.

We

make

butterflies.

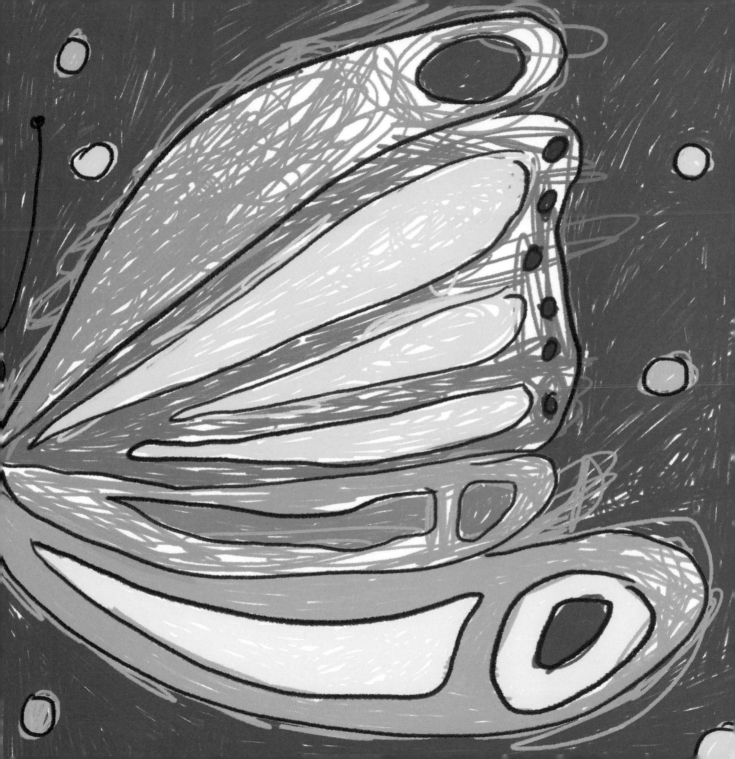

She
tells the
tooth fairy
not to
get lost.

front door

Help the tooth fairy
find her way from
the front door to
your pillow.

my room

my pillow

Add labels for
the rooms in
your home.

We go on

Find the
single scoop
of ice-cream
hiding on this page.

an ice-cream hunt.

She knows which colour I am

WHEN I'M HAPPY I'M

WHEN I'M SLEEPY I'M

WHEN I'M ANGRY I'M

WHEN I'M SAD I'M

WHEN I'M EXCITED I'M

WHEN I'M GRUMPY I'M

WHEN I'M SHY I'M

RAINBOW

on the inside.

ME

COME TO

She

bakes

the

best

MY PARTY

birthday

cake.

Decorate the birthday cake.
Don't forget to add candles on top.

We

see

shapes

in

the

clouds.

♥ What shapes can you see?

is my favourite letter.

♥ Circle all the words for Mum you know.

Moeder   Mëmë   Mam

Mum   Mãe   Majka   Mare

Muoji   Mor   Maminka   Máti

Muter   Morsa   Mère   Moeder

Maji   Mana   Makuahine

Mom   Màthair   Mamma   Mutter

Mater   Mótina   Mor   Madre

Maică   Mai   Matka   Mātā

Mama   Majka   Matka   Me

I
love
my
mum
because

she's the best mum
for me.

My hand

♥ Trace around your hand.

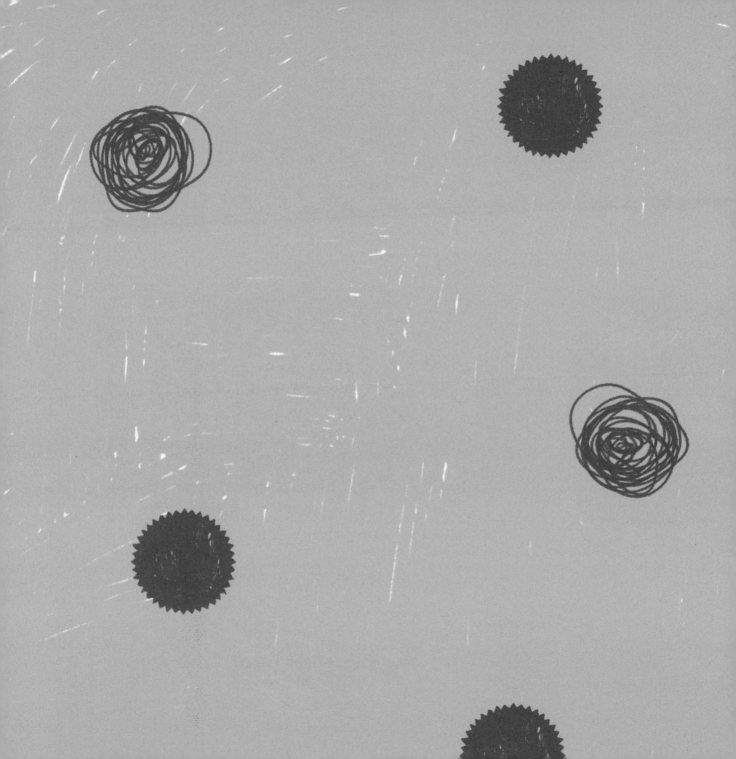